RHYTHMS

of

RENEWAL

ALSO BY REBEKAH LYONS

Freefall to Fly

You Are Free
(book, video curriculum, and study guide)

Rhythms of Renewal
(book, video curriculum)

RHYTHMS of RENEWAL

STUDY GUIDE | FIVE SESSIONS

REBEKAH LYONS

WITH KEVIN AND SHERRY HARNEY

ZONDERVAN®

ZONDERVAN
Rhythms of Renewal Study Guide
Copyright © 2019 by Rebekah Lyons

Requests for information should be addressed to:
Zondervan, *3900 Sparks Dr. SE, Grand Rapids, Michigan 49546*

ISBN 978-0-310-09885-0 (softcover)
ISBN 978-0-310-09886-7 (ebook)

Author is represented by The Christopher Ferebee Agency, www.christopherferebee.com.

Cover design: Curt Diepenhorst
Cover illustration: Dana Tanamachi
Interior design: crosslincreative.net

First Printing September 2019 / Printed in the United States of America

CONTENTS

HOPE ON THE HORIZON

Have you found yourself trapped in addiction? Feelings of unworthiness? Loneliness? Depression? Isolation? Consumerism? Rejection? Image management? If so, know this: God makes a way of escape. Rescue is ready and waiting, but so often, we are unwilling to take a closer look. We get lost in our loops, engage in the same habits over and over again expecting different results.

What do you do when anxiety hits, when it throbs in your ribs or steals your breath? When your words race and you try a desperate attempt to yawn and fill your lungs? What do you do when this is the norm of your everyday life? What do you do when relapse hits? Silence settles, distraction fades and you face panic, depression, or anxiety again? What do you do when you descend into anxiety after being panic-free for years?

These are the questions many of us are asking these days. According to the American Institute of Stress ("AIS"), 77 percent of the population experience physical symptoms associated with stress on a regular basis, 33 percent report living with extreme stress, and 48 percent indicate stress has a negative impact on their personal and professional lives.[1] The AIS estimates the aggregate cost to employers of stress-related healthcare expenses and missed work is $300 billion annually.[2] What's more, according to the National Alliance of Mental Illness ("NAMI"), 18 percent of American adults currently suffer from an anxiety disorder. Some estimate over 35 percent of the population will experience an anxiety disorder in their lifetime.[3] The NAMI indicates nearly 7 percent of the population struggles with chronic depression.[4]

This is why this five-session study is so important. As a society, we are in the throes of a collective panic attack. We nurse anxiety-chasing careers, hunger for security, and strive to keep up. We're afraid we're not doing enough. We obsess over health, politics, and a host of other things we can't control. That's when fatigue takes over. Fear rises. Finally, despair prevails.

As long as there is darkness in this world, we'll be tempted to be anxious and fearful. But over and over Scripture tells us not to fear. Jesus said, with piercing clarity, "Do not let your hearts be troubled and do not be afraid" (John 14:27).

The command not to fear is given over three-hundred times in the Bible (some say 365 times, once for every day of the year). In fact, it's a phrase used more than any other command in the Bible.

Here is the good news. With a little intentional effort, stress and anxiety can be traded for peace and purpose. It won't happen overnight, but it will happen. It might not be easy, but it can become your reality. That is what this five-session study is all about.

There are four biblical, God-given rhythms that help us replace fear with faith. They can teach us to nurture and sustain lasting mental health. These rhythms aren't complicated. Each can be expressed in one word: ***Rest***, ***Restore***, ***Connect***, and ***Create***. These rhythms take practice. Simple acts like fasting from media (Rest), exercising (Restore), sharing a laugh (Connect), or recovering an old talent (Create) can help us break the anxiety-inducing cycles of the world around us. They can bring balance to our otherwise hectic lives. They will help us cultivate the spiritual and mental space needed to allow God to bring us past fear and into freedom.

These four rhythms fit naturally into the flow of life. The first two—***Rest*** and ***Restore***—are "input rhythms," rhythms that allow the peace of Jesus to fill us. The latter two—***Connect*** and ***Create***—are "output rhythms," which pull us out of our own heads and connect us to the world around us.

My hope and prayer is that five or ten years from now you'll look back on your own season riddled with anxiety and see how God brought you to a place of health and peace through the rhythms of renewal outlined in this video-based Bible study. Please join me in praying that this journey of learning in a small community of people will transform your life and theirs.

A fellow traveler on the road to renewal,

Rebekah Lyons

OF NOTE

The study introduction and quotations interspersed throughout this study guide are excerpts from the book *Rhythms of Renewal* and the video curriculum of the same name by Rebekah Lyons. All other resources including the session introductions, small group questions, prayer direction, and between-sessions materials have been written by Kevin and Sherry Harney in collaboration with Rebekah Lyons.

SESSION

1

LIVING
in
RHYTHM

We all face moments, weeks, months, or even years when anxiety and panic come crashing into our lives. Thankfully, God has provided simple rhythms to help us navigate these times and come through with greater health, peace, and even joy.

INTRODUCTION

Group leader, read the introduction to the group before showing the video for this session.

Lin was always an energetic, passionate, joyful girl. All through grade school she made friends easily, excelled in her classes, and even had time for sports and fun activities. At the core of her life was a deep and authentic love for Jesus and for the people in her life. You might say that things just came easily for Lin.

That is why her parents were surprised and confused when her transition to high school was so difficult. Fear seemed to move into her heart overnight and confidence evaporated. Where she had been peaceful, anxiety took hold. Within a few weeks this was impacting her physical well-being, her sleep patterns, and the condition of her skin. In addition, her relationships changed as she pulled into herself and began avoiding friends.

God is in the business of pushing back the darkness.

Lin and her parents talked and prayed about all she was experiencing. There did not seem to be any major event that caused these problems. It just all descended unannounced and uninvited. Lin's parents assured her that God was with her and Jesus was ready and able to help her through this confusing and painful time.

Cynthia had been married for more than a decade and loved being a wife, mom, and using her many gifts to serve others. She had always struggled with anxiety, worry, and fears. She had learned to press down these feelings, hold them back, stay busy, and manage them. She figured this was just the way life worked. Her mom, in a number of honest conversations, had told Cynthia that the women in their family "all dealt with this kind of thing." So, she pressed on, tried not to complain, and lived with her pain.

Then, the dam broke. Over the course of a busy and intense December, with lots of family responsibilities, infrequent sunshine, and stress over finances, Cynthia realized she could not hold back the fears and anxiety. Like a wave, for the first time, all these feelings came to the surface and it was almost paralyzing. All she could do was look up and cry out to Jesus, "Help me, I can't handle my own life."

TALK ABOUT IT

What are some of the things in our world that are causing anxiety and worry in the hearts of people?

_____

_____

or

Tell about a person you love and care about who knows Jesus but has still dealt with anxiety. How did their anxiety impact their life and those around them?

_____

_____

*The rhythms of renewal
help sustain us emotionally,
spiritually, relationally,
and even vocationally.*

Meaning follows surrender   Jesus I come under
bravery moving scared   Your covering of peace.

TEACHING NOTES VIDEO SESSION 1

As you watch the teaching segment for this session, use the following outline to record anything that stands out to you.

Concepts modeled in Scripture . . . Rest, Restore, Connect, Create

Rest

Our spiritual life — what God wants to do

Restore

our physical life

Connect

our social life

Create

our vocational life

Input Rhythms . . . Fill me, Lord

Rest & Restore inventory life honest before God

Output Rhythms . . . Use me, Lord

Connect with other

God Created with Rhythm . . . Evening, morning, and another day

recover our passion

Genesis 1

From the beginning God followed a pattern of rhythm: Day and night, land and sea, earth and sky, sun and moon, light and dark.

Genesis 1:1-~~5~~13

Examples of Rhythm

1 Corinthians 10:13

when tempted - gives a way out
common to man   meet you there and equip you
not meant to harbor pain -

The Example of Jesus . . . A life of rhythm

Luke 5:15–16

Jesus rested - ordered by God
needed input rhythm

Luke 6:12–16

Jesus was restored

Connect . . . The one whom Jesus loved, Lazarus

walked talked dined -

Parables . . . The Sower, Prodigal Son

Created - painting a visual understanding

4 seeds- how each of us receive His word   run live our own ⟩ Prodigal
way our own will ⟩ Son

*When we follow God's
rhythm, it leads to
more rhythm.*

work of Jesus is reconcilation
through the rhythms

GROUP DISCUSSION

1. Tell about a time when anxiety, worry, or fear came crashing into your life uninvited and unexpected. How did this impact your life?

2. How does rhythm bring peace and calm in a world that can feel out of control and haphazard? Tell about one rhythm (of any kind) in your life that gives birth to peace and calm.

 *God created rhythm.*

3. *Group leader, look up and read aloud the following passage or invite a volunteer to do so:* **1 Corinthians 10:13.**

   Temptations, stress, hard times, and anxiety are part of life. They can throw us out of rhythm. Tell about a time when you got out of rhythm due to a stressful or difficult situation. What did it take to get your rhythm back and find peace again?

   > *When we face anxiety and stress, these are not shocking exceptions, they are just part of life.*

4. *Group leader, look up and read aloud the following passages or invite a volunteer to do so:* **Luke 6:12–13** and **Exodus 20:8–11.**

   Why do you think God takes rest and refreshment so seriously? What is one step you can take to make regular rest a consistent part of your life?

*God pours into us in the still
and silent places so he can pour
us out in the world he loves.*

5 *Group leader, look up and read the following passage or invite a volunteer to do so:*
1 Corinthians 6:19–20.

It is easy to become overextended and forget to care for our bodies. Why do you think God is concerned that we are careful to restore our bodies and tend to our physical health? What is one step you could take toward physical restoration in your life?

6 We live in a radically connected world where many people feel less connected than ever. How did Jesus reveal the importance of connecting when he walked on this earth? What can you do to connect in more regular and meaningful ways with the people God places in your life?

7 God spoke and all things came into existence. Jesus spoke with creativity and unleashed fresh vision and heavenly truth. What are ways we can be more creative with our words, our time, and our God-given abilities?

*Learn to say these words
from the depths of your
soul: "Jesus, I come under
your covering of peace."*

CLOSING PRAYER

Spend time in your group praying together. The group leader may pray over the group or ask for volunteers. Below are some suggested prayer prompts:

Thank God for calling you to rest, being an example of rest, and making rest part of the rhythm of life.

Ask God to give you discipline to follow his rhythm of restoration as you seek to honor him with how you care for your body.

Invite the Holy Spirit to take you to deeper places of connecting with the people God has placed in your life.

Ask Jesus to unleash the creative potential he has placed in you in fresh, new, beautiful ways.

Pray for the members of your group to step fully and joyfully into these rhythms over the coming weeks as you meet together.

> *In times of anxiety and worry,*
> *try saying this, "Jesus . . .*
> *Jesus . . . Jesus . . . Jesus!"*

WRAP-UP

Group leader, read the following wrap-up as you close your group.

What a joy to learn about how God created the whole universe with rhythm built into the very fabric of our world and lives. Let's all do our best to make time, before we meet again, to engage in some of the exercises provided here in our study guide. Also, as we prepare for the next time we gather, seek to notice how well you rest, or what keeps you from resting.

Key Scriptures: I Corinthians 10:13, Luke 5:15-16, Luke 6:12-16, Exodus 20:8-11, I Corinthians 6:19-20

This week's Study: Rhythms of Renewal Study Guide Session 1, Book reading: Introduction

Next week: Session Two: Rest

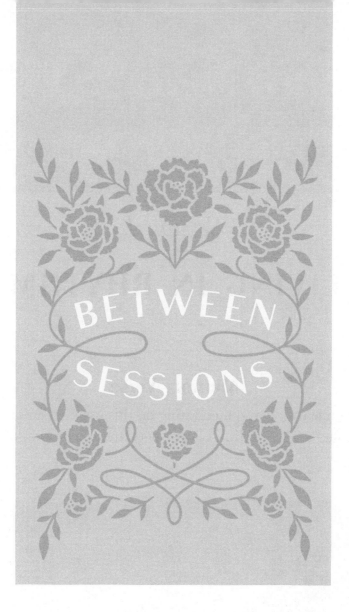

BETWEEN SESSIONS

*Make time in three days of the coming week to go deeper into **Rhythms of Renewal** by using the resources provided here in your study guide. If you take your time to do these exercises slowly and reflectively each day, it should take about 20–30 minutes.*

PERSONAL STUDY

Session 1

LIVING IN RHYTHM

 Day 1

Memory Verse

Take time to begin learning and meditating on this week's memory verse. Reflect on how God created with a rhythm of creativity and celebration of the goodness of what he made.

> *God saw all that he had made, and it was very good. And there was evening, and there was morning—the sixth day.*
>
> **(Genesis 1:31)**

Let Wisdom Speak

Take time to make a list of three to five people whose spiritual lives you respect and appreciate. These are not perfect people, but they have a deep, rich, authentic relationship with Jesus. They find rest and spiritual strength in their Savior.

Names:

1. Elaine Hannula

2. Bonnie Benford

3. Brenda Remick

4. Bob Remick

5. Sandy Coelho

Write down three or four things about these people that you have noticed in terms of how they find rest in their faith, how they connect to Jesus, and spiritual life-patterns they engage in:

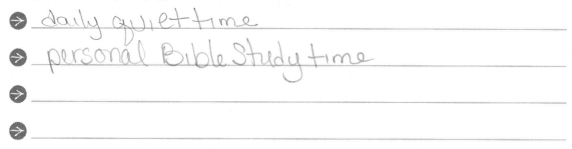

➔ daily quiet time

➔ personal Bible Study time

➔

➔

If you are able to, contact a couple of these people and ask them if they will share their personal patterns, spiritual habits, their rhythms of renewal that help them find rest and strength through Jesus. Write down what you learn in the space on the next page:

_____

_____

Finally, set one personal goal for a rhythm of rest that you can establish in your life and practice in the coming thirty days. Ask at least one trusted Christian friend to pray for you, keep you accountable, and cheer you on for the coming month.

My rhythm for spiritual rest and refreshment:

_____

_____

_____

Who I have asked to pray for me and encourage me:

_____

_____

_____

*We rarely recognize how much
we rely on rhythm because
God has built it into us.*

Day 2

Memory Verse

Continue learning and meditating on this week's memory verse. Reflect on the rhythm of a normal day with morning and evening.

> *God saw all that he had made, and it was very good. And there was evening, and there was morning—the sixth day.*
>
> **(Genesis 1:31)**

Rhythm of Restoration

Take time to pray about one restorative habit you can develop in the coming thirty days that will propel you forward in physical health and refreshment. It can be a time of stretching, daily exercise, refraining from certain foods, a commitment to getting to bed at a certain time, not snacking after a set time in the evening, or some other practice. The key is identifying something that you can do daily and that is attainable.

My practice for the coming thirty days:

_____

_____

_____

Make a commitment to pair this time with prayer, listening to worship music, being quiet, or interacting with a Christian you love and respect.

Keep a journal of how this practice makes you feel and impacts your life over the next four weeks.

Observations:

_____

_____

_____

_____

_____

_____

_____

_____

_____

_____

_____

In times of darkness and worry, God will stand alongside you and give you everything you need.

Day 3

Memory Verse

Solidify your memory verse by meditating on the words, speaking them out loud, and thinking of the goodness of God's creation.

> *God saw all that he had made, and it was very good. And there was evening, and there was morning—the sixth day.*
>
> **(Genesis 1:31)**

Learning from the Creativity of Jesus

In Matthew 13, Jesus tells a series of stories called parables. In each one we see the creativity of our Savior and discover how he weds together truth and memorable stories. Take time to read three of these stories, noting the truth contained in the parable and the creative way Jesus reveals this truth.

STORY 1: *The Parable of the Weeds* (Matthew 13:24–30, 36–43)

The truth I learn from this story:

_____

_____

_____

_____

What I learn about the creativity of Jesus:

_____

_____

_____

_____

How this story can impact my life as I follow Jesus:

_____

_____

_____

_____

_____

_____

STORY 2: *The Parable of Hidden Treasure* (Matthew 13:44–46)

The truth I learn from this story:

What I learn about the creativity of Jesus:

How this story can impact my life as I follow Jesus:

STORY 3: *The Parable of the Net* (Matthew 13:47–52)

The truth I learn from this story:

_____

_____

_____

_____

What I learn about the creativity of Jesus:

_____

_____

_____

_____

How this story can impact my life as I follow Jesus:

_____

_____

_____

_____

_____

_____

Journal

Use the space provided below to write some reflections on the following topics:

➡ What steps can I take to make meaningful and consistent rest part of a normal week?

_____

_____

_____

_____

➡ What is getting in the way of my developing life-patterns that lead to physical restoration, and how can I remove these barriers?

_____

_____

_____

_____

➡ What is one joy-giving, life-giving, creative pursuit that I used to engage in but do not anymore? How might I make this more a part of my life in the coming months?

_____

_____

_____

_____

God says, "I care more about your presence than your performance."

Recommended Reading

As you reflect on what God is teaching you through this session, you may want to read the introduction to *Rhythms of Renewal*.

SESSION

2

REST

Jesus was God in human flesh, the Almighty Maker of heaven and earth, and he still rested. If Jesus made room for a rhythm of rest, how much more should we?

INTRODUCTION

Group leader, read the introduction to the group before showing the video for this session.

Who needs a nap?

Who needs a day off?

Who needs to slow down and take a deep breath?

The truth is, we all do. God made us for hard work and meaningful engagement . . . no question. But God also created us with a need for rest, refreshment, and moments when our souls are recharged and renewed. Rest is so central to the human experience that Jesus built in a rhythm of rest into the days, weeks, months, and years of his life. Our Savior slipped away from the crowds and demands and found quiet time with his Father.

Ponder that reality for a moment.

Jesus was Immanuel, God with us. He was perfect God and perfect man. Yet, he still made rest a cornerstone of his life. It was a priority.

Where did our Lord learn this sacred rhythm? He learned it from his Father. As God was creating the heavens and earth, after six days of glorious, epic, artistic work, he rested. The infinite Yahweh took a day off! The Almighty ceased his labor. The Creator of you and me showed his children how to live. Let's follow his example and make rest part of our lives.

God ordained and blessed rest.

Who needs a nap, a day off, a chance to breathe deeply? Every one of us. Resting and establishing a rhythm of refreshment is not about weakness; it is about being more like Jesus. It is about honoring our Creator. Rest is about living with wisdom, learning from our Father, and walking in the footsteps of our Savior.

TALK ABOUT IT

What gets in the way of you living a rested life that is punctuated by moments of quiet and soul-filling refreshment?

_____

_____

_____

_____

or

What has helped you develop a rhythm of rest, and how has this pattern made your life better?

_____

_____

_____

_____

 Rest precedes blessing.

TEACHING NOTES VIDEO SESSION 2

As you watch the teaching segment for this session, use the following outline to record anything that stands out to you.

A Moment of Tragedy . . . When rest is needed most

Social Media . . . There are times to shut it down, fast, and take a break

lost true voice

invitation to bring back to source of creativity

The Fruit of a Social Media Fast:

Fresh Dreams

original thoughts - new excitement

Restful Sleep

phone other side of house

Recovered Time   learn again

how much time we waste online

God Ordained Rest . . . And called it good

ordained + blessed —

rest preceeds blessing

Sabbath not optional

Jesus Modeled Rest . . . Lessons from the Savior Mt 14: 13-14

Jesus always retreated

Rest requires pursuit. rest needs to be important to us I meet God in the Prayer room and the pulpit. Solitude is w/God

The Value of a Morning Routine . . . Like Jesus, Abraham, David, Moses, and Joshua
Gen 19:27 Ps 119:47   Ps 5:3
Jos 3:1

Mark 1:35   God wakes up early - pray journal Thank Him what He has planned for the day. ①Get Quiet Examine. ② Take Inventory of Life
Ps 139:23-24

A Life-Giving Practice . . . Confessing and Releasing

What Right? Wrong? Confused? Missing?

3) Confess & Release   not meant to be our own savior

Rest is not a sign of weakness it is a sign of meekness.

GROUP DISCUSSION

1 Tell about a time you faced loss, pain, or unexpected turmoil in your life. How did this challenging time impact your rhythm of rest?

2 If we are totally honest, what are some ways that social media can impact our lives in an unhealthy way? What do you think might happen if you were to take an extended break from social media?

Sometimes, instead of sharing, we are copying, competing, and comparing.

3 *Group leader, look up and read aloud the following passage or invite a volunteer to do so:* **Exodus 20:8–11.** If you have a rhythm of rest every seven days, tell about what you do during this Sabbath time and paint a picture of how this rhythm of rest helps you stay healthy and close to Jesus.

Sabbath is not optional; it is mandated.

4 *Group leader, look up and read aloud the following passage or invite a volunteer to do so:* **Mark 1:35.** If you have a daily morning time with God that helps set the direction for your day, tell about it.

*Jesus invites us to come,
get away with him, and
recover our lives.*

5 What is the difference between experiencing deep rest in our souls and just vegging out and seeking to escape from life? What are examples of ways we veg out and seek to disconnect that don't really refresh or recharge our souls?

*Real rest leads to real
replenishment.*

6 *Group leader, look up and read aloud the following passage or invite a volunteer to do so:* **Matthew 14:6–14.** What happened that moved Jesus to get away and find a place of quiet and rest? What are some of the hard life experiences that you have faced (or are facing) that make times of solitude, rest, and refreshment even more important. How can your group members pray for you and support you when you face a time like this?

7 How can confessing and releasing our burdens, sin, and guilt to God help us find deep and lasting rest? Why do we cling to these things rather than releasing them to the God who loves to heal and forgive? How can your small group members pray and support you as you seek to do this?

CLOSING PRAYER

Spend time in your group praying together. The group leader may pray over the group or ask for volunteers. Below are some suggested prayer prompts:

⟳ Thank God for giving you an example of rest, even from the beginning of time and the creation of the world.

⟳ Pray for the courage and power to shut off distractions (even your phone and social media) so that you can find places of deep and lasting rest.

⟳ Invite the Spirit of God to meet you in new, fresh, life-giving ways as you seek to develop times and places of rest.

⟳ Confess the ways you are drawn to run too hard, work too much, and stay too connected. Ask God to help you confess and release the things that hold you in the bondage of unrest.

You cannot run if you cannot rest.

WRAP-UP

Group leader, read the following wrap-up as you close your group:

Rest is a gift, not a punishment! We were made for rest, and our loving God is ready to give us this gift, when we are ready to receive it. Let's commit to develop habits and rhythms of rest that set us free and refresh us to the very core of our being. And, as we prepare for the next time we meet, let's note what we do to restore our physical health and vitality, and also the things that get in the way of us thriving in our physical health.

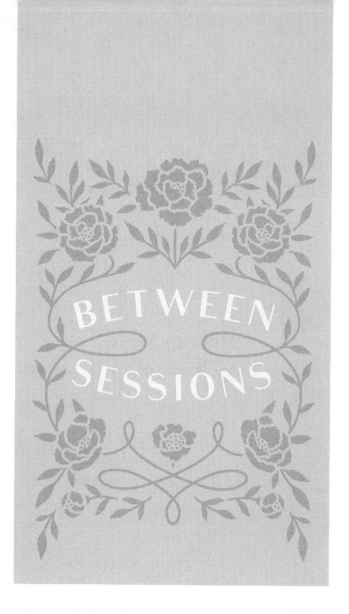

BETWEEN
SESSIONS

*Make time in three days of the coming week to go deeper into **Rhythms of Renewal**
by using the resources provided here in your study guide. If you take your time to do
these exercises slowly and reflectively each day, it should take about 20–30 minutes.*

PERSONAL STUDY

Session 2

 Day 1

Memory Verse

Take time to begin learning and meditating on this week's memory verse. Reflect on how Jesus made time with the Father a priority.

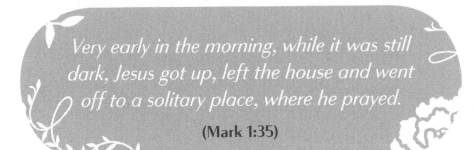

Very early in the morning, while it was still dark, Jesus got up, left the house and went off to a solitary place, where he prayed.

(Mark 1:35)

 Scripture is about meditating day and night.

Tech Detox

Take a tech and social media fast. You might want to do one day, a few days, a week, or even longer. Make a commitment and let a few people who love you know what you are doing. They might just cheer when you tell them. Then, write down your goal in this study guide.

The length of my tech/social media fast: _____

The extent of this fast (What will I shut off, avoid, and stay away from?)

→ _____

→ _____

→ _____

Make a list of the effects of this fast. It can be good things that happen in you and the people around you, changes in your soul, transformed relationships, space for God, anything you notice. Take note of these effects in the space below:

→ _____

→ _____

→ _____

→ _____

→ _____

→ _____

At the end of your tech/social media fast, answer these five questions:

1 What did I miss?

_____

What didn't I miss?

_____

_____

 What positives do I assign to the use of technology in my life?

_____

_____

 What negatives do I assign?

_____

_____

 What is my next step in this area of my life, and how can I make adjustments that lead to greater rest and refreshment for the long haul?

_____

_____

 Share what you learned and goals you made with a trusted friend and move forward with a new level of rest in your life.

_____

_____

When I shut off social media, I began to dream new dreams.

Day 2

Memory Verse

Continue learning and meditating on this week's memory verse. Think about when and where Jesus went for this time of rest, and then identify times and places you can get away with the Savior.

> *Very early in the morning, while it was still dark, Jesus got up, left the house and went off to a solitary place, where he prayed.*
>
> **(Mark 1:35)**

Get Quiet . . . Listen Well

We can't listen while we are talking. When we get quiet, slow down, and notice the people around us, rest and depth can enter our relational world. Try this simple (but challenging exercise) over the coming week.

When you are with a friend or family member and engaged in a conversation, work intentionally at these three things:

1. **Listen** closely. This means talking less and even seeking to stop thinking about what you will say next. Just listen. Ask genuine questions about their life, joys, hurts, and dreams. Listen to their heart, not just their words. As you do this, let yourself feel what they feel and even quietly pray for them as you are listening.

2. **Discern** deeply. Seek to hear what they mean and want to say but don't actually put into words. Learn to read between the lines and discern what is deep in their heart. When you do talk and respond, you might even talk about what you discern and not just what you hear. Pay attention to body language, facial expressions, and the subtle tone in their voice.

⑤ Understand as best you can. Being quiet and really listening to people is not about us getting ready to launch into what we want to say or to talk about ourselves. It is about having real empathy for them, loving well, and gaining insight to their joy, pain, and longings.

Use the space below to collect a few thoughts and insights that you gain as you learn to get quiet and listen at a whole new level.

Person and when I had this conversation: _____

Fresh new insights and understanding that came as I got quiet and listened deeply:

→ _____

→ _____

→ _____

Person and when I had this conversation: _____

Fresh new insights and understanding that came as I got quiet and listened deeply:

→ _____

→ _____

→ _____

Person and when I had this conversation: _____

Fresh new insights and understanding that came as I got quiet and listened deeply:

→ _____

→ _____

→ _____

*It takes humility to surrender
to God's order of rest.*

Day 3

Memory Verse

Solidify your memory verse by meditating on the words, speaking them out loud, and thinking of the importance of receiving the gift of rest in your life.

> Very early in the morning, while it was still dark, Jesus got up, left the house and went off to a solitary place, where he prayed.
>
> **(Mark 1:35)**

Stop the Work

Sabbath is more than stopping our work. It is ceasing our labor so we can focus on the things that matter most.

In the coming week, make space for a day, or three to five hours, of Sabbath. As you prepare for this time of rest and refreshment, think about three things you can do:

Reconnect with *God*:

_____

_____

_____

Reconnect with *Family*:

_____

_____

_____

Reconnect with your *Community*:

_____

_____

_____

Write down a few things you discovered about yourself as you made a time of Sabbath rest part of your week:

→ _____

→ _____

→ _____

→ _____

→ _____

The plans I have for you begin from a posture of rest.

Journal

Use the space provided below to write some reflections on the following topics:

 What would a healthy, life-giving, joy-filled day of rest look like? What can I do to take meaningful steps toward this kind of rhythm of Sabbath?

_____

_____

_____

_____

 What keeps me from quiet and rest, and how can I remove some of the rest distractions I face on a regular basis?

_____

_____

_____

_____

> *Your value as a human being isn't found in what you produce; it's found in who you are in Christ.*

Recommended Reading

As you reflect on what God is teaching you through this session, you may want to read Part 1 of *Rhythms of Renewal.*

SESSION

3

RESTORE

Once we have embraced the consistent rhythm of rest we find the potential of being restored. This means being physically replenished, mentally fortified, and emotionally engaged. Rhythms of restoration lead to health and vitality in all of our lives.

INTRODUCTION

Group leader, read the introduction to the group before showing the video for this session.

In the classic poem, *Touch of the Master's Hand*, we read the story of an old, forgotten, seemingly worthless violin that is placed on the auction block. No one is interested. There are no buyers. Then, to everyone's surprise, an old man comes forward, picks up the violin, and plays it. The sound is beautiful, powerful, gripping. The next moment, the whole scene changes. The bidding for this same instrument goes out the roof. Everyone wants the violin.

Years ago, this simple poem was turned into a song that became very popular. The reason is clear to see. When the Master takes something into his hands, his touch changes everything. We are the violin and Jesus is the Master. His touch restores our brokenness and his presence in our lives changes everything. Jesus is ready to pick us up, dust us off, and make us more beautiful than we have ever dreamed.

In the Gospel accounts recorded in the New Testament, Jesus shows us what a restored life looks like. He gives us an example, a vision to follow. Do you long for physical restoration and refreshment in your body? Would you delight to experience emotional restoration and a new picture of who you are and who you can become? Would you love to have your mind sharper than ever and your soul activated by the presence of the Holy Spirit? Jesus is waiting to do all of this and more.

In this session we will invite the Master artist and Savior to pick us up and show all of us exactly who we are and all we can become in his power. Brace yourself. Restoration comes from Jesus, and he is with you right now.

Jesus, I want to feel joy, I want to enjoy your creation, and I want to relax into your will.

TALK ABOUT IT

How has Jesus restored your body, heart, soul, or some other part of your life?

_____

_____

_____

_____

or

What is one area of life in which you long to experience restoration, and how can your group members pray for you as you seek Jesus' restoring power and presence?

_____

_____

_____

_____

We are a people in desperate need of restoration.

TEACHING NOTES VIDEO SESSION 3

As you watch the teaching segment for this session, use the following outline to record anything that stands out to you.

A Horse Story . . . Being stretched beyond fear

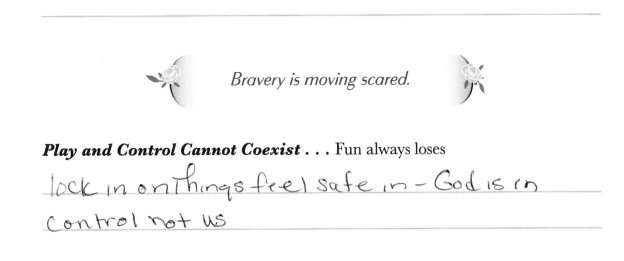

Bravery is moving scared.

Play and Control Cannot Coexist . . . Fun always loses

lock in on things feel safe in - God is in control not us

Somewhere on the journey from childhood to adulthood we can start to take control and only do what seems safe to us.

A Vision of Restoration . . . Isaiah 58:11–12

want a new life - we are in need of restoration don't discard make livable again

The Example of Jesus . . . How the Son of Man practiced rhythms of renewal

Jesus walked (physical activity)

walked over 3,000 miles in His ministry

Jesus practiced outdoor restoration

behold new things

Jesus' diet would have been healthy food from the earth

go back to simplicity of Bible
body is temple take care of it plant based diet

Jesus strengthened his mind

 Study of Scripture

Ask questions

 Our thought life (understanding our identity)

Writers are readers

> *When we read the Bible or other great books, and get lost in it, it sharpens our minds.*

The Story of Cade . . . Labels should never define us

labels don't define us - once know
someone don't go back to labelling
them.
He will be my way of escape

I am a new creation

I am a child of God, a friend of Jesus, I am created by God to do good, I am free In Christ, I am chosen and loved, I am not ruled by fear, I am secure in him, I am loved by God.

Gal 2:20

GROUP DISCUSSION

 Tell about a time you relaxed, played, and found amazing delight in something you experienced. How can trying to completely control our environment actually stifle fun and limit the joy of play?

*Play and control cannot **co-exist**.*

2 *The group leader will read the following passage aloud to the group:*

Isaiah 58:11–12 (The Message).

> *I'll give you a full life in the emptiest of places—*
> *firm muscles, strong bones.*
> *You'll be like a well-watered garden,*
> *a gurgling spring that never runs dry.*
> *You'll use the old rubble of past lives to build anew,*
> *rebuild the foundations from out of your past.*
> *You'll be known as those who can fix anything,*
> *restore old ruins, rebuild and renovate,*
> *make the community livable again.*

Take a moment in quiet reflection and read the passage silently, thinking about your own life right now. What are your empty places; when do you need to feel physically stronger; how does your life need refreshing water poured on it; what part of your life needs to be rebuilt? Share one of these areas where you need restoration, and let your group members know how they can pray for you and cheer you on.

5 The first disciples of Jesus literally walked with him and met Jesus in the movement. What are practical ways we can encounter Jesus in the physical activity of a day? As a group, try to list at least a dozen.

1. _____

2. _____

3. _____

4. _____

5. _____

6. _____

7. _____

8. _____

9. _____

10. _____

11. _____

12. _____

Tell your group about one way you personally seek to encounter Jesus while being physically active, and share how you can increase both the activity and your connection with Jesus.

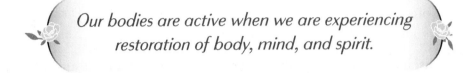

Our bodies are active when we are experiencing restoration of body, mind, and spirit.

4 How can good food and a healthy diet serve to restore our bodies and even help us maintain emotional and soul health? If we don't pay attention to what we eat, drink and put in our bodies, how can this hurt our physical, emotional, and soul health?

5 *Group leader, look up and read aloud the following passage or invite a volunteer to do so:* **Luke 2:41–50.**

How do we see Jesus developing his mind in the Gospel stories? What are ways we can develop our mind and strengthen it, and what are some of the behaviors and habits that actually weaken and damage our minds?

Habits that strengthen our mind:

_____

_____

_____

_____

_____

Behaviors that can weaken our mind:

_____

_____

_____

_____

_____

Tell your group about one habit you can stop and one you can start that will help you restore and strengthen your mind.

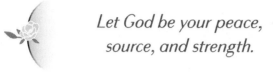

Let God be your peace, source, and strength.

6 What are some of the labels that people have tried to place on you or someone you love?

 Labels interrupt our rhythm.

7 *Group leader, look up and read aloud the following passages or invite a volunteer to read to do so:* **1 Peter 2:9–10** *and* **Galatians 2:20.** Why is it essential that we listen to the Scriptures and let God's Word define who we are? Who does God say you are and how should this define everything you think and do?

We must always put God above our label, diagnosis, or any scary thing we are facing.

CLOSING PRAYER

Spend time in your group praying together. The group leader may pray over the group or ask for volunteers. Below are some suggested prayer prompts:

→ Invite God to restore anything and everything in you that needs his divine and loving touch.

→ Thank God for the many ways he has already restored you, or is restoring you right now.

→ Ask for discipline and strength to keep renewing your mind through reading and meditating on the words of the Bible.

→ Thank God for calling you his child, his beloved, a friend, and so much more!

Behold and enjoy God's surprises along the way.

WRAP-UP

Group leader, read the following wrap-up as you close your group:

The world might give you a label, a diagnosis, or a name you never wanted. Here is the good news: the world is not the boss of you. You have a Savior who came to this world to offer you complete restoration. He wants to partner with you on the journey. He has already given you a perfect example to follow. He is with you and in you. And, he is the one who will pick you up, dust you off, and show you and the world just how valuable you are. Take time this week embracing rhythms of rest. Embrace the restoration Jesus wants for you. And prepare your heart for fresh new connections as you walk on this journey in a community of people who love God and care about you.

BETWEEN SESSIONS

Make time in three days of the coming week to go deeper into **Rhythms of Renewal** *by using the resources provided here in your study guide. If you take your time to do these exercises slowly and reflectively each day, it should take about 20–30 minutes.*

PERSONAL STUDY

Session 3

Day 1

Memory Verses

Take time to begin learning and meditating on this week's memory verses. Reflect on how God has restored your life and how he is presently restoring you.

> *I'll give you a full life in the emptiest of places—*
> *firm muscles, strong bones.*
> *You'll be like a well-watered garden,*
> *a gurgling spring that never runs dry.*
> *You'll use the old rubble of past lives to build anew,*
> *rebuild the foundations from out of your past.*
> *You'll be known as those who can fix anything,*
> *restore old ruins, rebuild and renovate,*
> *make the community livable again.*
>
> **(Isaiah 58:11–12, The Message)**

Making Space for Play

Often the inhibitor to play is control. We want to control our schedule, the tidiness of our home (or hair), or even the people around us. Decide to punctuate your days and weeks with play . . . even when this stretches you.

Identify some things you like to do, that you enjoy, or that you think might be fun (but you have never tried). List the ideas here:

→ _____

→ _____

→ _____

→ _____

→ _____

→ _____

→ _____

Decide to do one fun thing every other day for a week. This means you will do at least three fun things in a week's time. Keep a record of what you did, if you had fun, and if you would like to do it again.

What I did for fun: _____

Did I enjoy it? If so, why?

_____

_____

Will I do this again, and with whom?

_____

_____

What I did for fun: _____

Did I enjoy it? If so, why?

_____

_____

Will I do this again, and with whom?

_____

_____

What I did for fun: _____

Did I enjoy it? If so, why?

_____

_____

Will I do this again, and with whom?

_____

_____

If you find something that brings delight to your life and that restores your joy quotient, make it a rhythm in the flow of your life . . . and share it with others. They need to have fun too!

*It's play that breaks us out
of our stressful routines
and rejuvenates us.*

Day 2

Memory Verses

Continue learning and meditating on this week's memory verses. Reflect on areas you desire to experience restoration and pray for God to do his work in you.

> *I'll give you a full life in the emptiest of places—*
> *firm muscles, strong bones.*
> *You'll be like a well-watered garden,*
> *a gurgling spring that never runs dry.*
> *You'll use the old rubble of past lives to build anew,*
> *rebuild the foundations from out of your past.*
> *You'll be known as those who can fix anything,*
> *restore old ruins, rebuild and renovate,*
> *make the community livable again.*
>
> **(Isaiah 58:11–12, The Message)**

Make Margin for Healthy Eating

Try a seven-day experiment. Make some specific decisions about what you will eat (and your family, if this applies to you). Use the space below to identify your simple but important goals:

What we **will** eat:

_____

_____

_____

What we **won't** eat:

_____

_____

_____

When we will eat:

_____

_____

Keep a list of things that change because of these new rhythms (physical changes, emotional impact on you or family members, energy levels, etc.)

→ _____

→ _____

→ _____

→ _____

→ _____

What are some rhythms in my eating habits that I will continue as I go forward?

_____

_____

_____

*You are what you eat, so
what you put in comes out.*

Day 3

Memory Verses

Solidify your memory verses by meditating on the words, speaking them out loud, and asking God to use you as his agent of restoration in your home, church, community, and the world.

> *I'll give you a full life in the emptiest of places—*
> *firm muscles, strong bones.*
> *You'll be like a well-watered garden,*
> *a gurgling spring that never runs dry.*
> *You'll use the old rubble of past lives to build anew,*
> *rebuild the foundations from out of your past.*
> *You'll be known as those who can fix anything,*
> *restore old ruins, rebuild and renovate,*
> *make the community livable again.*
>
> **(Isaiah 58:11–12, The Message)**

I Am Who God Says I Am

Spend time reflecting on the following declarations God makes about you:

- I am a child of God (John 1:12).

- I am a new creation (2 Corinthians 5:17).

- I am a friend of Jesus (John 15:15).

- I am created by God to do good (Ephesians 2:10).

I am free in Christ (Galatians 5:1).

I am chosen and loved (1 Thessalonians 1:4).

I am the light of the world (Matthew 5:14).

I am not ruled by fear (2 Timothy 1:7).

I am forgiven (Colossians 2:13).

I am God's possession (Titus 2:14).

I am free from the desires of the flesh (Galatians 5:24).

I am a light in the world (Matthew 5:14–15).

I am secure in him (1 Peter 1:3–5).

I am loved by God (1 John 4:10).

Read each of these biblical truths slowly and silently.

Next, read each one slowly and thoughtfully, letting God's truth sink into your heart.

Next, read each out loud and boldly like a declaration from heaven.

Finally, call, text, or write a note to a Christian you care about and remind them who they are through faith in Jesus (use the above list to guide you).

 The abundant life that Jesus promised far exceeds the life I am living.

Journal

Use the space provided below to write some reflections on the following topics:

➡ What labels do I need to release, toss out, and be done with?

_____

_____

_____

_____

➡ What needs to be restored in my heart and life, and what rhythms will help me on the journey to restoration in this area?

_____

_____

_____

_____

➡ How might God use me to bring restoration to someone in my life in the coming days? How can I take action to partner with Jesus in his restoring work?

_____

_____

_____

_____

In this restored life I can repair walls, rebuild ruins, and make the community livable again.

Recommended Reading

As you reflect on what God is teaching you through this session, you may want to read Part 2 of *Rhythms of Renewal.*

SESSION

4

CONNECT

Once we have the input of Rest and Restore, and these rhythms mark our lives, we can begin to honor God as we let the output rhythms flow. We can connect with people in meaningful and life-giving ways. Our friendships, family relationships, and all of our human connections thrive. We were created for connection and when we move away from isolation and into community, God delights, and we feel the joy of God blessing others as we live with rhythms of connection.

INTRODUCTION

Group leader, read the introduction to the group before showing the video for this session.

Jesus did not leave the glory of heaven to institute a religious system and deliver a list of do's and don'ts. Our Savior did not come to build monuments to himself or commission the construction of massive cathedrals in his name. Jesus came to connect with real people in a real world with real love.

Think about it. When Jesus called the disciples, his primary concern was connection. In the third chapter of Mark we read:

Jesus went up on a mountainside and called to him those he wanted, and they came to him. He appointed twelve that they might be with him and that he might send them out to preach. Mark 3:13–14

Look closely at the biblical text and notice that Jesus called people to himself. This is a picture of intimacy. In response, they came to him. The people drew near Jesus. Finally, the motive of Jesus comes to the surface. Jesus appointed apostles that they might "be with him." This was the core priority of Jesus as he related to the apostles. It was all about connection.

Then, in the name of Jesus, the rest of the New Testament lifts up the sacred joy and privilege of being part of a community. We are called to live connected to each other. The pictures are as intimate as human language allows. We are to be like the parts of a human body, each belonging to the other (1 Corinthians 12; Romans 12). We are a family of faith who are members of the same household (Ephesians 2:19; 1 Timothy 5:1–2).

Connection with people is so foundational that in the very beginning of the Bible, God is clear that we were designed to be a connecting people. God exists in eternal Trinitarian community (Genesis 1:26). When he made Adam, God declared, "It is not good for the man to be alone" (Genesis 2:18). Connection is hard-wired into the soul of every human being. If we are going to be healthy and live in the will of the God who made us, we need to embrace the call to community and make connection a rhythm in our lives.

Even though we sometimes avoid human connection because we have so much going on, it is the thing we need more than anything.

TALK ABOUT IT

What erodes community and pushes you away from being connected with others?

_____

_____

or

Tell about a person in your life who engages regularly in a rhythm of connecting with others. What do you learn from the example of this person?

_____

_____

We have replaced face-to-face relationships with conversations online.

TEACHING NOTES VIDEO SESSION 4

As you watch the teaching segment for this session, use the following outline to record anything that stands out to you.

A Bag of Bows . . . Creative connection

Never meant to be alone. Cannot give what we do not receive.

Cultivating Friendships . . . Be the friend you wish to have

If you want to have friends you show yourself friendly

The power of hospitality

need to welcome people into home

Be creative

fun gatherings

Be in the trenches together

walk with one another

 Be a friend, be a blessing.

Put Your Phone Down . . . And spend time together

Family Connections . . . A great starting point

Marriage connections

pride arrogance
can't harbor bitterness seeds of resentment

Connection with your kids

listen and look at things
new challenges with each season change

> It is common, normal, and easy to avoid relating to people. The problem is, we will never experience full connection if we do this.

God's Word and Connections . . . Hebrews 10:24–25

dont overlook things   common to avoid getting
together—never experience fullness

Connect with God . . . This puts all other relationships in the proper perspective

when have good input with God—
everything comes together

Three Biblical Guidelines:

Lead with vulnerability

Someone has to do it

> In moments of vulnerability
> we find connection.

Bear with one another Col 3:13

Don't keep record of wrong

Say will do something but don't follow through

Love one another Jo 15:12-13

love with God's love

> *When we let relationships interrupt our lives, that's when we are starting to build true community and connection.*

GROUP DISCUSSION

 Why do we need the input rhythms of Rest and Restore before we can connect in meaningful ways? How might our relationships suffer if we don't practice the input rhythms?

 What are some creative or common ways you have learned to connect well with friends? What keeps your friendships fresh, live, and meaningful?

> *If we want a trusted friend, we need to be trustworthy.*

③ What do you look for in a good friendship, and how can you seek to be this kind of friend to others?

④ Why is being vulnerable and transparent essential for a deep and rich friendship? What are hindrances to vulnerability, and how can we overcome these?

Transparency is sharing where you have been; vulnerability is sharing where you are right now.

⑤ *Group leader, look up and read aloud the following passage or invite a volunteer to do so*: **Hebrews 10:23–25.**

What guidelines does this passage give us in terms of our connections in our relational world? How can you go deeper in one of these areas?

⑥ How does connecting deeply with God fuel and strengthen all of our other relationships? What are specific ways we can connect more deeply with God in ways that will grow our connections with the people in our lives?

The enemy wants to thwart relationships because he knows we are made for community.

7 *Group leader, look up and read aloud the following passage or invite a volunteer to do so:* **Colossians 3:12–14.**

If we lived with the attributes taught in this passage, how would this strengthen our relational connections? Who is someone you need to bear with and forgive (share without using a name)?

8 *Group leader, look up and read aloud the following passage or invite a volunteer to do so:* **John 15:12–13.**

What does it look like for us to be willing to lay down our lives for the people we love? What are ways we can do this and be more sacrificial as we love others?

 Walk through hard times together.

CLOSING PRAYER

Spend time in your group praying together. The group leader may pray over the group or ask for volunteers. Below are some suggested prayer prompts:

➡ Thank God for people who have loved you and invested in their relationship with you.

➡ Pray for power and grace to be the kind of friend you wish you had.

Ask God to give you courage to be vulnerable and transparent in your relationships with friends and family members.

 Ask the Holy Spirit to give you courage and strength to bear with people who have wronged and hurt you.

 Pray for a heart filled with love that is sacrificial and always ready to count the cost.

Collaborative creativity is the best kind and we can't create until we connect.

WRAP-UP

Group leader, read the following wrap-up as you close your group:

Once we are practicing the rhythms of Rest and Restore, we are filled up and healed enough to pour out some of the good things God is giving us. We can connect in meaningful ways that uplift others; we become a conduit of God's grace and goodness; and we watch as community forms all around us. When this happens, creativity begins to blossom. The life-giving presence of Jesus, released in the community of God's people, gives birth to new visions, dreams, and creative expressions that honor the Savior. As you seek deeper connections this coming week, take note of how the Holy Spirit begins to unleash creative expressions of grace all around you.

BETWEEN SESSIONS

Make time in three days of the coming week to go deeper into **Rhythms of Renewal**
by using the resources provided here in your study guide. If you take your time to do
these exercises slowly and reflectively each day, it should take about 20–30 minutes.

PERSONAL STUDY

Session 4

Day 1

Memory Verse

Begin learning and meditating on this week's memory verse. Reflect on how we are called to connect with other people and love them as Jesus has loved us. What kind of community could God unleash on the world if we loved this way?

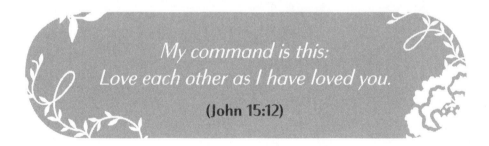

My command is this:
Love each other as I have loved you.

(John 15:12)

Be the Friend You Wish to Have

Take a few minutes to *reimagine your friendships*. What would they look like if you did the following things:

1 Trusted that God has placed these specific people in your life.

_____

_____

_____

2 Sought to be vulnerable and authentic.

_____

_____

_____

3 Sacrificed with a generous spirit.

_____

_____

_____

4 Extended forgiveness.

_____

_____

_____

Seek to implement one or more of these as you grow into the kind of friend you would like to have.

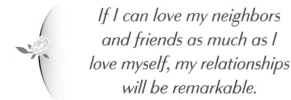

If I can love my neighbors and friends as much as I love myself, my relationships will be remarkable.

Memory Verse

Solidify your memory verse by meditating on the words, speaking them out loud, and thinking of ways you can connect more deeply with God and the people he has placed in your life.

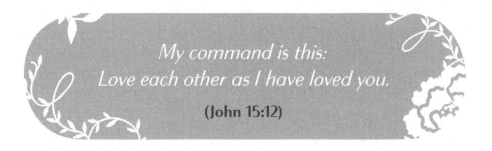

My command is this: Love each other as I have loved you.

(John 15:12)

Bear a Burden, Share a Burden

Many people will not open their heart and life to us until we do so with them. Take a moment and write down two or three burdens you are carrying right now. It could be your own burden or the burden of someone you love.

A Burden I Am Bearing:

_____

_____

A Burden I Am Bearing:

_____

_____

A Burden I Am Bearing:

_____

_____

Pray about which burden you can share with someone in your life. And, prayerfully reflect about whom you can share this burden with.

The Burden I Will Share:

_____

_____

The Person I Will Share With:

_____

Contact this person and ask if they would be willing to do three things as you share this burden:

Will they listen?

Will they pray for you right now, and in the coming days?

Will they encourage you and support you as you walk through this time?

If they are willing, share your heart with honest vulnerability. You will be amazed at how others will let you carry their burden if you will first invite them to help carry yours.

We weren't designed to bear our fears, our anxieties, our worries on our own.

 Day 3

Memory Verse

Repeat and meditate on this week's memory verse one more time. Reflect on how connection with Jesus and receiving his love is the starting point of lasting community.

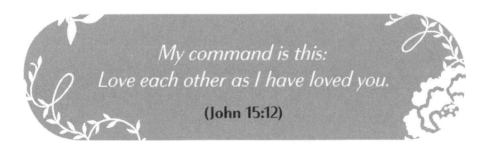

*My command is this:
Love each other as I have loved you.*

(John 15:12)

Say It . . . I'm Sorry

One of the biggest roadblocks to meaningful connection is unresolved conflict and brokenness that has not been healed.

Take time to identify one person with whom you are at odds right now. Write their name in the space below and describe briefly (without great detail) what has caused the conflict:

Name: _____

What is at the center of this tension?

_____

_____

Next, with this person in your heart, sing a song of worship. You can do it with just your voice or you can pull it up on YouTube or Spotify and sing along. Worship God as you think about this person and the broken connection you are experiencing. Now, write down where you have been wrong, resistant, prideful, or out of line in any way. What should you own in the broken relationship?

My part in the conflict:

→ _____

→ _____

→ _____

Set a time to meet with this person. Do all you can to make it happen. When you are together, be ready to do three things:

1. Tell them where you have been in the wrong and out of line. Express what you could have done better.

2. Apologize and ask for their forgiveness. Be ready to say you are sorry for your part.

⑤ Take a step forward to fresh connections in this relationship. Ask yourself and the other person, "When can we connect again?"

You might be thinking; this process is all about me. What about the other person? What about their apology?

You can't control them, but you can do the right thing. Your example might be just what they need to break free and ask for forgiveness from you. But, if they don't, you can know you have done the right thing to seek healing in the relationship.

The best response when connection is broken is not to push away, but rather the opposite, to pull in.

Journal

Use the space provided below to write some reflections on the following topics:

 What keeps me from forgiving and bearing with those who have hurt me? What can I do to extend the grace God has given to me in Jesus?

 Who are people I have not connected with in a long time and how can I rekindle those relationships?

_____

_____

_____

_____

_____

We need to make conscious decisions to talk about things we might want to dust under the rug.

Recommended Reading

As you reflect on what God is teaching you through this session, you may want to read Part 3 of *Rhythms of Renewal*.

SESSION

5

CREATE

In the beginning of all things, God was rested, restored, and in perfect community (connected) as Father, Son, and Holy Spirit . . . so, he created. When we have developed rhythms of Rest, Restore, and Connect, we are ready to develop rhythms of Create. God unleashes this as an output that helps build his kingdom, grow his church, and make us more like him.

INTRODUCTION

Group leader, read the introduction to the group before showing the video for this session.

Ask a hundred people, "Are you creative?" The vast majority will say, "No!"

Most of us look at ourselves and don't recognize the great potential for creativity that God has birthed in us. We think creative people are artists who can paint, sculpt, dance, sing, and maybe even make a living at their art. We see creativity as a limited commodity reserved for a small group of people.

This is a sad misunderstanding. God is the most creative being in the universe and each of us is a work of art. In addition, God calls us to be creative for his glory. We can express this in the way we raise children, how we interact with friends, how we do our work, cook a meal, deal with challenges, walk with Jesus, and a million other things. Creativity is expressed as we follow Jesus in our own unique way, out of the temperament, passion, dreams, and personality God has given us.

What gets in the way of us being creative is rarely the spark of creativity . . . God has placed this in all of us. The biggest roadblocks are a lack of rest (we are exhausted) or a lack of restoration (we feel empty). When the rhythms of Rest and Restore are part of our life, creativity begins to bubble up in surprising and fun ways.

Creating or cultivating something new gives us a sense of accomplishment and joy.

TALK ABOUT IT

Tell about a time you took a risk and tried something creative, really had fun, and felt God's joy fill you.

_____

_____

_____

_____

or

What is a creative thing you have always wanted to do but have never tried? What is keeping you from giving this a try?

_____

_____

_____

_____

 We experience life when we work with our hands and seek to foster creativity.

TEACHING NOTES VIDEO SESSION 5

As you watch the teaching segment for this session, use the following outline to record anything that stands out to you.

Growing Up in a Crafty Home . . . Beautiful examples

The Flow of the Rhythms . . . Rest, Restore, Connect lead to Create

Biblical Examples of Creating . . .

God the Father at the beginning

Jesus the craftsman

God the Master Craftsman . . . We are made for good works

*Jesus created and shared
what he made with others
as a way of life.*

God Calls Us to New Places of Creativity . . . Take risks and embrace it

Barriers to Creativity . . . Press past them

A Beautiful Example . . . A life immersed in the rhythms

Rhythms are cyclical by design.

GROUP DISCUSSION

1 Tell about a time you created something (a poem, a recipe, a model of something, a song, anything). How did you feel in the creative process and how did you feel when it was finished?

2 *Group leader, look up and read aloud the following passage or invite a volunteer to do so:* **Genesis 2:15.**

Early in Scripture God gives work as a good gift in perfect paradise before any sin exists. How is meaningful and creative work a gift from God? Tell about some kind of work you do, how you need to be creative as you do it, and how God is present in this creating process.

3 When Jesus taught, he was creating. He told stories, made up parables, and crafted creative images to bring alive deep and eternal truths. What is one of your favorite stories Jesus told (take a minute and look through the four Gospels)? How does this creative storytelling help you engage with God's truth for your life?

Little steps of faith that seem like a meandering path can be God's avenue to invite us into creativity.

4 *Group leader, look up and read aloud the following passages or invite a volunteer to do so:* **Ephesians 2:10** and **Exodus 35:10–15.**

God is all about creativity! Tell about one unique way God has created you . . . something about you that other people might not know? What is something God wants to create through you, and how can your group members pray for you and cheer you on as you seek to follow God's unique plan for your life?

5 Tell about a time God called you to a whole new season of life that demanded creativity, risk taking, and trust in him. How did you grow through that season?

God is not going to call you to something that doesn't require all of him.

6 It is essential to stay close to God as we seek to exercise the creativity he births in us. How can pride take over if we are successfully creative but do it on our own? How can fear and regret take over if we are unsuccessful in our creativity and doing it on our own? How does partnering with God in creative endeavors buffer us from both pride and fear?

The specific decision to obey can set us on a whole new trajectory.

7. What is one step toward creativity you believe God wants you to take (this can be big or small and in any area of your life)? How can your group members keep you accountable and support you as you take this step in partnership with Jesus?

CLOSING PRAYER

Spend time in your group praying together. The group leader may pray over the group or ask for volunteers. Below are some suggested prayer prompts:

➤ Thank God for the creative ways he has made you and shaped your life.

➤ Give God praise for the beauty of his creativity in you, in the people around you, and in the world he has made.

➤ Ask God to help you always give him praise for the creative gifts you have.

➤ Invite the Holy Spirit to draw you to fresh new places of creativity that will bring glory to God and strengthen his church.

Thanksgiving and praise
are matters of the will,
not our emotions.

WRAP-UP

Group leader, read the following wrap-up as you close your group:

We are coming to the close of an amazing journey, discovering the rhythms of renewal. We have been learning the input rhythms of Rest and Restore as well as the output rhythms of Connect and Create. But really, we are not ending but just beginning. These biblical and Spirit-led practices are meant to guide our lives from this day forward. So let's keep talking about them, praying for each other, and cheering each other on.

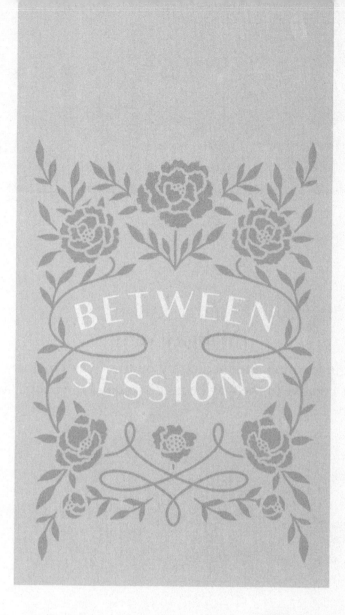

Make time in three days of the coming week to go deeper into **Rhythms of Renewal** by using the resources provided here in your study guide. If you take your time to do these exercises slowly and reflectively each day, it should take about 20–30 minutes.

PERSONAL STUDY

Session 5

Day 1

Memory Verse

Take time to begin learning and meditating on this week's memory verse. Reflect on how God was creative in the way he made you and the people around you.

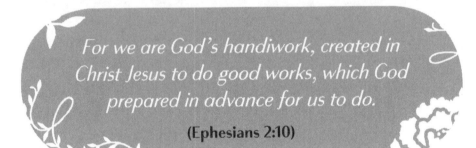

For we are God's handiwork, created in Christ Jesus to do good works, which God prepared in advance for us to do.

(Ephesians 2:10)

Learn Something New . . . Take a Class

One of the best ways to take a step forward in creativity is to learn something new. You may want to sign up for a class at your church, a community center, online, or at a local school. Walk through this process:

Pray about what creative endeavor God might have for you.

Here is what I sense from the Lord:

_____

_____

_____

Talk with a couple of friends and share what you are considering. Ask them what they think might be a good step for you.

What I hear from my friends:

_____

_____

_____

Do some online **research** about available options.

Ideas I found:

_____

_____

_____

Make a **decision** as to what class you will take and then have fun. Learn. Meet new people. And grow your creativity.

*God is always going to
invite us into things where
his glory is revealed and
his vision is fulfilled.*

Day 2

Memory Verse

Solidify your memory verse by meditating on the words, speaking them out loud, and thinking of ways you can be creative as you do the daily work and activities God has placed before you.

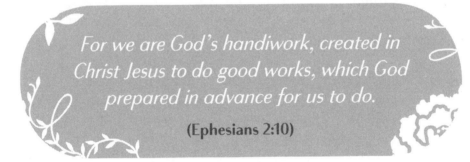

*For we are God's handiwork, created in
Christ Jesus to do good works, which God
prepared in advance for us to do.*

(Ephesians 2:10)

Lessons from Dad

There are certain Bible passages that seem to speak power and life into our souls in a unique and beautiful way. Rebekah's father passed on to her a Bible that collected some of the passages that lifted him up in hard times and gave direction in living for Jesus. These passages also give us direction in how to develop the output rhythms of connecting and creating.

Take time and read each passage slowing and prayerfully. Then, answer the questions after each passage.

John 1:12: *Yet to all who did receive him, to those who believed in his name, he gave the right to become children of God.*

Reflect:

How can the truth of this passage bring you (and others) comfort and confidence even in the hard times of life?

_____

_____

_____

When we receive the truth of this passage, how do we view the people around us who have placed their faith in Jesus and know God as Father? When we understand that other followers of Jesus are actually our brothers and sisters (children of God) beautifully created in his image, how does this help us connect more closely with them?

_____

_____

_____

Psalm 103:12: *As far as the east is from the west, so far has he removed our transgressions from us.*

Reflect:

How does this staggering truth bring comfort and hope when we are feeling burdened or down?

_____

_____

_____

How can a deep awareness that we are all forgiven sinners washed clean by the grace of God help us take risks as we create and try new things for Jesus?

_____

_____

_____

2 Timothy 1:7: *For the Spirit God gave us does not make us timid, but gives us power, love and self-discipline.*

Reflect:

 Sometimes we can feel discouraged and disheartened. How can the truth of this passage lift our spirits and help us move forward, even in tough times?

_____

_____

_____

 How could our personal creativity grow if we set aside timidity and embraced the power of Jesus?

_____

_____

_____

> *God has given you everything you need to fulfill his creative vision for your life.*

Day 3

Memory Verse

Continue learning and meditating on this week's memory verse. Reflect on some of the things God has created you to do.

> *For we are God's handiwork, created in Christ Jesus to do good works, which God prepared in advance for us to do.*
>
> **(Ephesians 2:10)**

Journal

Use the space provided below to write some reflections on the following topics:

→ What roadblock(s) to creativity am I facing and how can I get around it or remove it completely?

What new season is ahead of me, and how can God's creativity in me help me enjoy and be productive in this next chapter of my life?

_____

_____

_____

_____

_____

_____

_____

When we get comfortable and complacent it might just be time for a new and creative challenge.

Recommended Reading

As you reflect on what God is teaching you through this session, you may want to read Part 4 of *Rhythms of Renewal*.

SMALL GROUP LEADER HELPS

If you are reading this, you have likely agreed to lead group through *Rhythms of Renewal*. Thank you! What you have chosen to do is important, and much good fruit can come from studies like this. The rewards of being a leader are different from those of participating, and we hope you find your own walk with Jesus deepened by this experience.

Rhythms of Renewal is a five-session study built around video content and small-group interaction. As the group leader, imagine yourself as the host of a dinner party. Your job is to take care of your guests by managing all the behind-the-scenes details so that as your guests arrive, they can focus on each other and on interaction around the topic.

As the group leader, your role is not to answer all the questions or reteach the content—the video, book, and study guide will do most of that work. Your job is to guide the experience and cultivate your small group into a kind of teaching community. This will make it a place for members to process, question, and reflect—not receive more instruction.

There are several elements in this leader's guide that will help you as you structure your study and reflection time, so follow along and take advantage of each one.

BEFORE YOU BEGIN

Before your first meeting, make sure the participants have a copy of this study guide so they can follow along and have their answers written out ahead of time. Alternately, you can hand out the study guides at your first meeting and give the group members some time to look over the material and ask any preliminary questions. During your first meeting, be sure to send a sheet of paper around the room and have the members write down their name, phone number, and email address so you can keep in touch with them during the week.

Generally, the ideal size for a group is between eight to ten people, which ensures everyone will have enough time to participate in discussions. If you have more people, you might want to break up the main group into smaller subgroups. Encourage those who show up at the first meeting to commit to attending the duration of the study, as this will help the group members get to know each other, create stability for the group, and help you know how to prepare each week.

Each of the sessions begins with an opening illustration, which the leader can read or summarize. The choice of questions that follow serve as an icebreaker to get the group members thinking about the topic at hand. Some people may want to tell a long story in response to one of these questions, but the goal is to keep the answers brief. Ideally, you want everyone in the group to get a chance to answer, so try to keep the responses to a minute or less. If you have talkative group members, say up front that everyone needs to limit his or her answer to one minute.

Give the group members a chance to answer, but tell them to feel free to pass if they wish. With the rest of the study, it's generally not a good idea to have everyone answer every question—a free-flowing discussion is more desirable. But with the opening icebreaker questions, you can go around the circle. Encourage shy people to share, but don't force them.

Before your first meeting, let the group members know that each session contains three days' worth of Bible study and reflection materials that they can complete during the week. While this is an optional exercise, it will help the members cement the concepts presented during the group study time and encourage them to spend additional time in God's Word on their own. Also invite them to bring any questions and insights they uncovered while reading to your next meeting, especially if they had a breakthrough moment or if they didn't understand something.

WEEKLY PREPARATION

As the leader, there are a few things you should do to prepare for each meeting:

- *Read through the session.* This will help you to become familiar with the content and know how to structure the discussion times.

- *Decide which questions you definitely want to discuss.* Based on the amount and length of group discussion, you may not be able to get through all the questions, so choose four to five questions that you definitely want to cover.

- *Be familiar with the questions you want to discuss.* When the group meets, you'll be watching the clock, so you want to make sure you are familiar with the questions you have selected. In this way, you'll ensure you have the material more deeply in your mind than your group members.

- *Pray for your group.* Pray for your group members throughout the week and ask God to lead them as they study his Word.

- *Bring extra supplies to your meeting.* The members should bring their own pens for writing notes, but it's a good idea to have extras available for those who forget. You may also want to bring paper and additional Bibles.

Note that in many cases there will no one "right" answer to the question. Answers will vary, especially when the group members are being asked to share their personal experiences.

STRUCTURING THE DISCUSSION TIME

You will need to determine with your group how long you want to meet each week so you can plan your time accordingly. Generally, most groups like to meet for either sixty minutes or ninety minutes, so you could use one of the following schedules:

SECTION	60 minutes	90 minutes
Introduction (members arrive and get settled; leader reads or summarizes introduction)	5 minutes	10 minutes
Talk About It (discuss one of the two opening questions for the session)	10 minutes	15 minutes
Video Notes (watch the teach material together and take notes)	15 minutes	15 minutes
Group Discussion (discuss the Bible study questions you selected ahead of time)	25 minutes	40 minutes
Closing Prayer (pray together as a group and dismiss)	5 minutes	10 minutes

As the group leader, it is up to you to keep track of the time and keep things moving along according to your schedule. You might want to set a timer for each segment so both you and the group members know when your time is up. (Note that there are some good phone apps for timers that play a gentle chime or other pleasant sound instead of a disruptive noise.)

Don't be concerned if the group members are quiet or slow to share. People are often quiet when they are pulling together their ideas, and this might be a new experience for them. Just ask a question and let it hang in the air until someone shares. You can then say, "Thank you. What about others? What came to you when you watched that portion of the video?"

GROUP DYNAMICS

Leading a group through *Rhythms of Renewal* will prove to be highly rewarding both to you and your group members. However, this doesn't mean you will not encounter any challenges along the way! Discussions can get off track. Group members may not be sensitive to the needs and ideas of others. Some might worry they will be expected to talk about matters that make them feel awkward. Others may express comments that result in disagreements. To help ease this strain on you and the group, consider the following ground rules:

- When someone raises a question or comment that is off the main topic, suggest you deal with it another time, or, if you feel led to go in that direction, let the group know you will be spending some time discussing it.

- If someone asks a question you don't know how to answer, admit it and move on. At your discretion, feel free to invite group members to comment on questions that call for personal experience.

- If you find one or two people are dominating the discussion time, direct a few questions to others in the group. Outside the main group time, ask the more dominating members to help you draw out the quieter ones. Work to make them a part of the solution instead of the problem.

- When a disagreement occurs, encourage the group members to process the matter in love. Encourage those on opposite sides to restate what they heard the other side say about the matter, and then invite each side to evaluate if that perception is accurate. Lead the group in examining other Scriptures related to the topic and look for common ground.

When any of these issues arise, encourage your group members to follow these words from the Bible: "Love one another" (John 13:34), "If it is possible, as far as it depends on you, live at peace with everyone" (Romans 12:18), and "Be quick to listen, slow to speak and slow to become angry" (James 1:19). This will make your group time more rewarding and beneficial for everyone who attends.

NOTES

1. "What Is Stress," *The American Institute of Stress*, https://www.stress.org /daily-life.

2. "The Source of Your Stress," *Forbes Magazine* (website) https://www.forbes .com/sites/cywakeman/2013/06/20/the-source-of-your-stress/#4999f9c97626.

3. Borwin Bandelow and Sophie Michaelis, "Epidemiology of Anxiety Disorders in the 20th Century," *Dialogues in Clinical Neuroscience* 17 no.3 (September 2015): 327–335, https://www.ncbi.nlm.nih.gov/pmc/articles/PMC4610617/.

4. "Depression," *National Alliance on Mental Illness*, https://www.nami.org /Learn-More/Mental-Health-Conditions/Depression.

Rhythms of Renewal

Trading Stress and Anxiety for a Life of Peace and Purpose

Rebekah Lyons

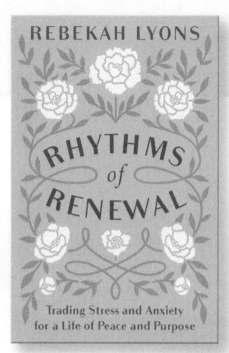

Daily struggles with anxiety and stress make it difficult to receive God's peace. In *Rhythms of Renewal*, beloved author Rebekah Lyons draws from her own battle with depression and anxiety and shares a pathway to establish four life-giving rhythms that quiet inner chaos and make room for a flourishing life.

As a society, we are in the throes of a collective panic attack. Anxiety and loneliness are on the rise, with 77% of our population experiencing physical symptoms of stress on a regular basis. We feel pressure chasing careers, security, and keeping up. We worry about health, politics, and many other complexities we can't control. Eventually we find our minds spinning, trying to cope or manage a low hum of anxiety, unlike ever before.

But it doesn't have to stay this way. With deep warmth, Rebekah welcomes you into an intentional, lifelong journey toward sustained emotional, relational, and spiritual health. *Rhythms of Renewal* is your guide to daily rescue and a way forward into the peace and purpose your soul longs for.

With heartening stories, research, and practical steps to take action, Rebekah charts a path through four profound rhythms to cultivate the vibrant life you were meant to live. By taking time to rest, restore, connect, and create, you will discover how to:

- Take charge of your emotional health and inspire your loved ones to do the same
- Overcome anxiety by establishing daily habits that keep you mentally and physically strong
- Find joy through restored relationships in your family and community
- Walk in confidence with the unique gifts you have to offer the world

Available in stores and online!

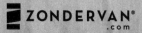

Also from Rebekah Lyons

In this six-session video Bible study, Rebekah Lyons helps you to reject the lie that what others think of you determines your worth. Jesus whispers, "I gave my life to set you free. I gave you purpose. I called you to live in freedom in that purpose." Christ doesn't say you can be or may be or will be free. He says you are free.

Study Guide
9780310085614

DVD
9780310085638

Book
9780310345527

Available now at your favorite bookstore,
or streaming video on StudyGateway.com.

BIBLE STUDY
SOURCE
for women
powered by ChurchSource

Connecting you with the best in

BIBLE STUDY RESOURCES

from many of the world's

MOST TRUSTED BIBLE TEACHERS

REBEKAH LYONS   MARGARET FEINBERG   ANN VOSKAMP   CHRISTINE CAINE

Providing

**WOMEN'S MINISTRY LEADERS,
SMALL GROUP LEADERS, AND INDIVIDUALS**

with the

INSPIRATION, ENCOURAGEMENT, AND RESOURCES
every woman needs to grow their faith in every season of life

powered by ChurchSource

join our
COMMUNITY

Use our BIBLE STUDY FINDER to quickly find the perfect study for your group,
learn more about all the new studies available, and download FREE printables
to help you make the most of your Bible study experience.

BibleStudySourceForWomen.com

FIND THE *perfect* BIBLE STUDY
for you and your group in 5 MINUTES *or* LESS!

Find the right study for your women's group
by answering four easy questions:

1. WHAT TYPE OF STUDY DO YOU WANT TO DO?

- *Book of the Bible:* Dive deep into the study of a Bible character, or go through a complete book of the Bible systematically, or add tools to your Bible study methods toolkit.

- *Topical Issues:* Have a need in a specific area of life? Study the Scriptures that pertain to that need. Topics include prayer, joy, purpose, balance, identity in Christ, and more.

2. WHAT LEVEL OF TIME COMMITMENT BETWEEN SESSIONS WOULD YOU LIKE?

- *None:* No personal homework
- *Minimal:* Less than 30 minutes of homework
- *Moderate:* 30 minutes to one hour of homework
- *Substantial:* An hour or more of homework

3. WHAT IS YOUR GROUP'S BIBLE KNOWLEDGE?

- *Beginner:* Group is comprised mostly of women who are new to the Bible or who don't feel confident in their Bible knowledge.

- *Intermediate:* Group has some experience with studying the Bible, and they have some familiarity with the stories in the Bible.

- *Advanced:* Group is comfortable with the Bible, and can handle the challenge of searching the Scriptures for themselves.

4. WHAT FORMAT DO YOU PREFER?

- *Print and Video:* Watch a Bible teacher on video, followed by a facilitated discussion.

- *Print Only:* Have the group leader give a short talk and lead a discussion of a study guide or a book.

Get Started!
Plug your answers into the **Bible Study Finder**, and discover the studies that best fit your group!

Check out the Bible Study Finder at:
BibleStudySourcForWomen.com